1-30-75

In these twenty-two poems, black people speak out on pride and love—feelings about life and the future. The talents of new young poets are combined with masterworks by Gwendolyn Brooks, Langston Hughes, Nikki Giovanni, and others, resulting in a medley that carries the reader beyond the protest and anger of the 1960's into the 1970's—a time when all Americans are rethinking the country's future.

Lee Bennett Hopkins has used poetry with people of many backgrounds and ages from pre-school children to adults. The poems selected for this volume are those that have evoked special feelings from a vast number of audiences throughout America.

As Augusta Baker states in her Introduction: "We are black, we are proud, and we are on our way."

ON OUR WAY

Poems of Pride and Love / Selected by Lee Bennett Hopkins / Photographs by David Parks

Alfred A. Knopf ❧ New York

THIS IS A BORZOI BOOK PUBLISHED BY ALFRED A. KNOPF, INC.

Text copyright © 1974 by Lee Bennett Hopkins. Illustrations copyright © 1974 by Alfred A. Knopf, Inc.

All rights reserved under International and Pan-American Copyright Conventions. Published in the United States by Alfred A. Knopf, Inc., New York, and simultaneously in Canada by Random House of Canada Limited, Toronto. Distributed by Random House, Inc., New York. Designed by Elliot Epstein. Manufactured in the United States of America.

Library of Congress Cataloging in Publication Data

Hopkins, Lee Bennett, comp.   On our way; poems of pride and love.

Contents: Blackness: Zealy, Y. A prayer. Evans, M. Who can be born black. Porter, L. As a basic. Rice, J. N. You and me.— Soul love: Randall, D. Love poem. Patterson, R. R. A love song. Evans, M. If there be sorrow. Prettyman, Q. Lullaby. [etc.] 1. American poetry—Negro authors. [1. American poetry—Negro authors]   I. Parks, David, 1944- .   illus. II. Title. PS591.N4H6   811′.5′408   73-15112   ISBN 0-39-82773-2   ISBN 0-394-92773-7 (lib. bdg.)

for
Robert O. Boord
for
many things

L. B. H.

Contents

REMEMBERING

ON OUR WAY

Introduction

Historically, the most popular literary form among black Americans has been poetry. Dudley Randall, black poet-publisher, feels that "it is not only because it is the fastest and least expensive to create and reproduce, but also because it is in the black oral tradition." The black poet expresses his frustration, anger, love, and hope through his poetry and in so doing he speaks for all his people. The young person who reads this poetry feels these intense emotions and responds to them accordingly. He relives the black experience and relates to it.

The 1960's saw an upsurge of poetry that reflected the black man's disillusionment, bitterness, anger, and growing militancy. Pent-up emotions spilled forth and the black poet spoke directly to black folk about black folk. Race pride was in its ascendancy and black was beautiful. This was not an intellectual approach but rather it was an emotional one coming from the poet's soul. Black poets were putting it all together and putting it all down. Some people were shocked with the outspoken language but the poets knew that they must speak in the language of the day if they wished to relate to the people. True poetry deals not alone with beauty and goodness and the poetic vocabulary is not always refined and polite.

Anger and protest were at their peak in the sixties. Blacks were on their way. Poetry of the 1970's seems to say "We're not going to make it *one day*, we already have. We're here!"

Linda Porter says:

"Be Black, be Proud,
You're Basic."

Mari Evans says:

"Who
can be born
black
and not exult!"

We are black, we are proud, and we are on our way. We are here and here we will remain.

Today's youth, black and white, need to be reminded of this. The poems in this collection will not only remind young people of the past but, more importantly, they will point them to the future. There is power to do this in these poems. Today's fine young poets are expressing their new excitement with directness, intelligence, poetic sense, and honesty. The poems in this collection have all of these qualities and so they speak directly to children and young people. It is good to have a collection presented to young readers which conveys this excitement and relevance. One hopes that teachers, librarians, parents, will share these poems with our children so that new poets and writers will be born.

Augusta Baker
Coordinator,
Children's Service Division,
New York Public Libraries

BLACKNESS

A Prayer

Color me black, my Lord, as dark as ebony;
make my skin smooth as polished opal,
but toughen it so that the blows that
will rain upon it, will not leave it scarred.
Give me hair that is woolly and coarse
and nearly as black as my skin.
Bless me with teeth that are straight and white,
with a tongue that is sharp and clever.
Make my lips thick and soft;
press my nose to my face till it is broad and flat.
Bestow upon me, oh Lord, a body that is strong
and willful.
Give me all this, Lord, and then thrust me
naked into the world.
I am a Negro and I am proud.

YOLANDE ZEALY

Who Can Be Born Black

Who
can be born black
and not
sing
the wonder of it
the joy
the
challenge

Who
can be born
black
and not exult!

MARI EVANS

As a Basic

Black is a Basic, you can wear it with almost anything—
Pink, yellow, blue, tan, green, red—
Almost everyone has something Black to call his own:
Black eyes, Black hair, Black skin—Black hearts—
Why just yesterday, I noticed how black you were becoming.
And personally, I rejoiced at how beautifully you were turning
   Black.

The Essence of Blackness—that's You!
Ace of Spades, and Beautiful!!!
Don't tell me that you don't want to be Black!
Why man, that's the color to dig!
Be Black, be Proud,
You're Basic.

LINDA PORTER

You and Me

I saw a rose and it soothes my soul.

A black rose!
That rose was black as coal.

It was looking sweet and smelling fine,
I had an urge to make it mine.

I went to pick it, when lo and behold
That rose began to speak.

Look here, brother . . .
That rose did say,

I am black just like you.
Think before you break my back.
And, listen while I give you a clue.

For so many years we've been smelling foul,
Just garbage in one gutter or another.

When something black is finally smelling sweet,
You want to commit this low-down feat!

You are selfish, man!

That's what you are.
You want the honey dripping just on your star.

Let me stay!

I beg you, please!
So my sweetness can reach every man.
Then and only then place me in any one hand.

I looked and smiled and thought a while.

I bent down low and gently sighed . . .
Sweet black rose . . . bye . . . bye.

No one will know except you and me . . .
How sweet black can be.

JO NELL RICE

SOULLOVE

Love Poem

Love lover beloved love one
lovely lovelier loveliest lovable love
love loveless lovelorn lovelone lovelack lacklove
unloved misloved disloved underloved subloved
lovingkindness lovingcare tenderlove dearlove
sweetlove kindlove heartlove soullove
lovelily lovingly lovedlily lovably
lovelook lovetouch lovespeech lovetalk
closelove lightlove nightlove dawnlove
morninglove freshlove lovecalls lovecries
love love love love love love love
relove overlove surlove superlove
everloving heavenlove soullove heartlove truelove
loveosity lovefeats lovefeast lovefest
loveniks lovadors lovathons longlove lastinglove
lovability lovingness reloved surloved superloved
loveliness lover beloved loved one love done
love you love you love you love you

DUDLEY RANDALL

If There Be Sorrow

If there be sorrow
let it be
for things undone
undreamed
    unrealized
        unattained

to these add one:
love withheld
    restrained

MARI EVANS

15

A Love Song

Do I love you?
I'll tell you true,

Do chickens have lips?
Do pythons have hips?

Do penguins have arms?
Do spiders have charms?

Do oysters get colds?
Do leopards have moles?

Does a bird cage make a zoo?
Do I love you?

RAYMOND RICHARD PATTERSON

17

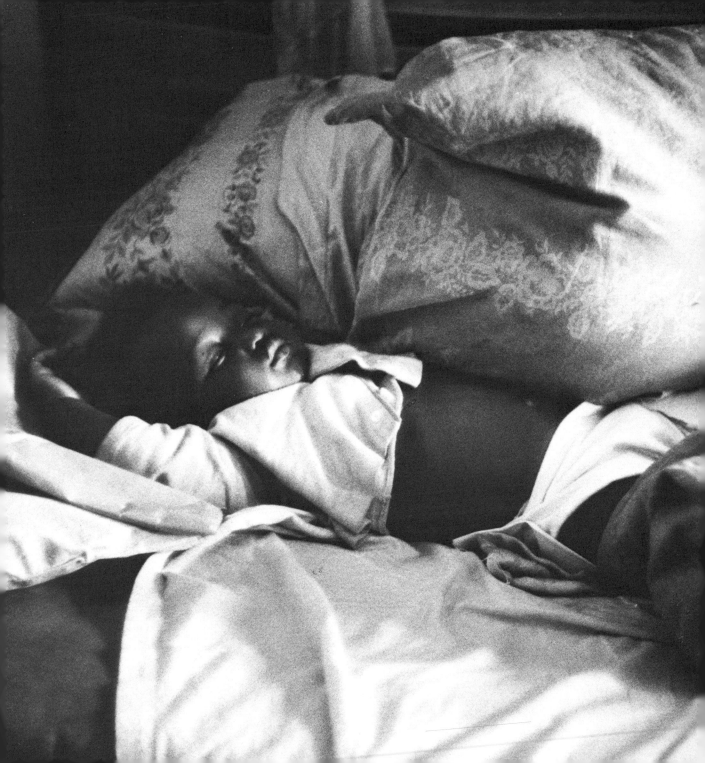

Lullaby

sleep, love, sleep,
just such peace
as you seem
to lie in
there to dream
is my least
gift, love, sleep.

sleep, love, sleep,
while I watch
here close by,
no harm comes,
rest easy,
good dreams catch
you, love, sleep.

sleep, love, sleep,
no thing brings
me greater
comfort than
being here
while your thoughts
sleep, love, sleep.

QUANDRA PRETTYMAN

FOUR

Gertrude

When I hear Marian Anderson sing,
I am a STUFFless kind of thing.

Heart is like the flying air.
I cannot find it anywhere.

Fingers tingle. I am cold
And warm and young and very old.

But, most, I am a STUFFless thing
When I hear Marian Anderson sing.

For Nina Simone Wherever You Are

The great
  singer
    Nina Simone
 fills your heart with soul
 she makes your brain rock and roll
 makes your mind forget
    the question that is unanswered

Go ahead Nina bring
  out all of your black soul
 Just sing it
  hit it to the
  white man eyes
 Make him realize
 that a black woman voice
   will never
    die

LINDA CURRY

Old Lang Hughes

Old Lang Hughes was a good friend of mine,
We'd talk on the corner nearly all the time.
We just sat on the stoop and talked all the time,
When the weather was bad and when the weather was fine.
I was smart but he was smarter, I'd say,
Boy, that old man used to talk my brains away.
We'd sometimes talk for weeks, then we'd flip;
Then the very next day I'd make another library trip.
And although he's dead, you will still find
Me standing and talking to him all the time!

MAURICE SHELLEY JACKSON

Martin's Blues

He came apart in the open,
the slow motion cameras
falling quickly
neither alive nor kicking;
stone blind dead
on the balcony
that old melody
etched his black lips
in a pruned echo:
We shall overcome
some day—
Yes we did!
Yes we did!

MICHAEL S. HARPER

FEELINGS

African in Louisiana

I stopped deep
In Louisiana once,
A cop close at my heels:

What! Go to the colored side.
Don't sit here!

Somewhat angry,
But, indeed, hungry,
I could only say:
Some day we will meet again,
Your heart changed
For friendship.

I sat, though,
And was served soup
In a miracle-whip bottle
I still keep
For a keepsake.

KOJO GYINAYE KYEI

Me, Colored

Aunt Liza.
Yes?
What am I?
What are you talking about?
I met a boy at the river.
He said he was Zulu.
    She laughed.
You are Colored.
There are three kinds of people:
White people, Colored people,
and Black People.
The White people come first,
then the Colored people,
then the Black people.
Why?
Because it is so.

Next day when I met Joseph,
I smacked my chest and said:
    Me, Colored!
He clapped his hands and laughed.

Joseph and I spent most
of the long summer afternoons together. . .
Our days were full.
There was the river to explore.
There were my swimming lessons.
I learnt to fight with sticks . . .
to weave a green hat
of young willow wands and leaves;
to catch frogs and tadpoles
with my hands.
There was the hot sun to comfort us.
There was the green grass to dry our bodies.
There was the soft clay with which to build.
There was the fine sand with which to fight.
There were our giant grasshoppers to race.
There were the locust swarms
when the skies turned black
and we caught them by the hundreds.
There was the rare taste of crisp,
brown-baked, salted locusts.
There was the voice of the wind in the willows.
There was the voice of the heavens
in the thunder storms.
There were the voices of two children
in laughter, ours.
There were Joseph's tales of black kings
who lived in days before the white man.

35

At home, I said:
Aunt Liza.
Yes?

Did we have Colored kings before the white man?
No.
Then where did we come from?
Joseph and his mother come from the
black kings who were before the white man.

Laughing and ruffling my head, she said:
You talk too much. Go'n wash up.

The Cure All

The summer is
coming.

CONGRESS HAS ACTED:

money into the
ghetto,

to keep the weather
cool.

DON L. LEE

Midway

I've come this far to freedom and I won't turn back.
I'm climbing to the highway from my old dirt track.
    I'm coming and I'm going
    And I'm stretching and I'm growing
And I'll reap what I've been sowing or my skin's not black.

I've prayed and slaved and waited and I've sung my song.
You've bled me and you've starved me but I've still grown strong.
    You've lashed me and you've treed me
    And you've everything but freed me
But in time you'll know you need me and it won't be long.

I've seen the daylight breaking high above the bough.
I've found my destination and I've made my vow;
    So whether you abhor me
    Or deride me or ignore me,
Mighty mountains loom before me and I won't stop now.

REMEMBERING

Knoxville, Tennessee

I always like summer
best
you can eat fresh corn
from daddy's garden
and okra
and greens
and cabbage
and lots of
barbecue
and buttermilk
and homemade ice-cream
at the church picnic
and listen to
gospel music
outside
at the church
homecoming
and go to the mountains with
your grandmother
and go barefooted
and be warm
all the time
not only when you go to bed
and sleep

NIKKI GIOVANNI

Sketches of Harlem

3.
The boy arrived from Mississippi
And got a room on Seventh Avenue the same day.
Right away he wrote to Mama:
   "Dear Ma,
       I got up here safely.
   I got me a room in Harlem
   and everything is all right."

DAVID HENDERSON   47

Nikki-Rosa

childhood remembrances are always a drag
if you're Black
you always remember things like living in Woodlawn
with no inside toilet
and if you become famous or something
they never talk about how happy you were to have your mother
all to yourself and
how good the water felt when you got your bath from one of
those big tubs that folk in chicago barbecue in
and somehow when you talk about home
it never gets across how much you
understood their feelings
as the whole family attended meetings about Hollydale
and even though you remember
your biographers never understand
your father's pain as he sells his stock
and another dream goes
and though you're poor it isn't poverty that
concerns you
and though they fought a lot
it isn't your father's drinking that makes any difference
but only that everybody is together and you
and your sister have happy birthdays and very good christmasses
and I really hope no white person ever has cause to write
about me because they never understand Black love is Black
wealth and they'll probably talk about my hard childhood
and never understand that all the while I was quite happy

NIKKI GIOVANNI

49

Daybreak in Alabama

When I get to be a composer
I'm gonna write me some music about
Daybreak in Alabama
And I'm gonna put the purtiest songs in it
Rising out of the ground like a swamp mist
And falling out of heaven like soft dew.
I'm gonna put some tall tall trees in it
And the scent of pine needles
And the smell of red clay after rain
And long red necks
And poppy colored faces
And big brown arms
And the field daisy eyes
Of black and white black white black people
And I'm gonna put white hands
And black hands and brown and yellow hands
And red clay earth hands in it
Touching everybody with kind fingers
And touching each other natural as dew
In that dawn of music when I
Get to be a composer
And write about daybreak
In Alabama.

LANGSTON HUGHES

Good Times

My Daddy has paid the rent
and the insurance man is gone
and the lights is back on
and my uncle Brud has hit
for one dollar straight
and they is good times
good times
good times

My Mama has made bread
and Grampaw has come
and everybody is drunk
and dancing in the kitchen
and singing in the kitchen
oh these is good times
good times
good times

oh children think about the
good times

LUCILLE CLIFTON

Where the Rainbow Ends

Where the rainbow ends
There's going to be a place, brother,
Where the world can sing all sorts of songs,
And we're going to sing together, brother,
You and I, though you're white and I'm not.
It's going to be a sad song, brother,
Because we don't know the tune,
And it's a difficult tune to learn.
But we can learn, brother, you and I.
There's no such tune as a black tune.
There's no such tune as a white tune.
There's only music, brother,
And it's music we're going to sing
Where the rainbow ends.

RICHARD RIVE

Acknowledgments

Grateful acknowledgment is made to the following for permission to reprint copyrighted material:

Broadside Press for "The Cure All" by Don L. Lee, from *Black Pride*, copyright © 1968 by Don L. Lee. Reprinted by permission of Broadside Press.

Mari Evans for "If There Be Sorrow" and "Who Can Be Born Black" from *I Am a Black Woman* by Mari Evans, published by William Morrow & Co., copyright © 1970. Reprinted by permission of Mari Evans.

Michael S. Harper for "Martin's Blues."

Harper & Row, Publishers, Inc. for "Gertrude" from *Bronzeville Boys and Girls* by Gwendolyn Brooks, copyright © 1956 by Gwendolyn Brooks Blakely. Reprinted by permission of Harper & Row, Publishers, Inc.

Holt, Rinehart & Winston, Inc. for "For Nina Simone Wherever You Are," by Linda Curry; from *The Voice of the Children*, collected by June Jordan and Terri Bush, copyright © 1969 by The Voice of the Children, Inc. Reprinted by permission of Holt, Rinehart & Winston, Inc.

Indiana University Press for "Me, Colored" by Peter Abrahams; "African in Louisiana" by Kojo Gyinaye Kyei; "Where the Rainbow Ends" by Richard Rive; from *Poems from Black Africa*, edited by Langston Hughes, copyright© 1963. "Sketches of Harlem: 3" by David Henderson; from *New Negro Poets*; *U.S.A.*; edited by Langston Hughes, copyright 1964. Reprinted by permission of Indiana University Press.

Alfred A. Knopf, Inc. for "Daybreak In Alabama" by Langston Hughes; from *Selected Poems of Langston Hughes*, copyright © 1948. Reprinted by permission of Alfred A. Knopf, Inc.

Naomi Long Madgett for "Midway," from *Star by Star* by Naomi Long Madgett; published by Harlo Press, copyright © 1965, 1970. Reprinted by permission of the author.

McGraw-Hill Book Company for "Old Lang Hughes" by Maurice Shelley Jackson; "As a Basic" by Linda Porter; "You and Me" by Jo Nell Rice; "A Prayer" by Yolande Zealy; from *Cry at Birth*, collected and edited by The Bookers. Copyright © 1971 by Merrel Daniel Booker, Sr., Erma Barbour Booker, Merrel Daniel Booker, Jr., and Sue Booker. Reprinted by permission of McGraw-Hill Book Company.

William Morrow & Co. for "Nikki-Rosa" and "Knoxville, Tennessee" by Nikki Giovanni: from *Black Feeling, Black Talk, Black Judgement* by Nikki Giovanni, copyright © 1968, 1970. Reprinted by permission of William Morrow & Co.

Raymond Richard Patterson for "A Love Song."

Dudley Randall for "Love Poem" by Dudley Randall; copyright © September, 1970 by *Black World*. Reprinted by permission of *Black World* and Dudley Randall.

Random House, Inc. for "Good Times" by Lucille Clifton; from *Good Times*, copyright © 1969 by Lucille Clifton. Reprinted by permission of Random House, Inc.

Quandra Prettyman Stadler for "Lullaby" by Quandra Prettyman.

Photographic services were provided by Diana Custom Film Lab, Inc., 21 West 46th Street, New York, N.Y.

Index of Titles and Authors

Index of First Lines

About the Poets

Peter Abrahams was born in Johannesburg, South Africa in 1919 and lived there until he was twenty years old. For a time he worked aboard ships, but soon his ambition turned toward writing. In the 1950's he was sent to the West Indies on a writing assignment and so loved Jamaica that he decided to live there.

The poem in this collection, "Me, Colored," is from his autobiography *Tell Freedom*. Besides writing poetry, he has written several novels.

Gwendolyn Brooks was born in Topeka, Kansas in 1917. She was raised, and still lives in Chicago, Illinois. Her first book of poetry, *A Street in Bronzeville*, appeared in 1945. In 1950 she won the Pulitzer Prize for Poetry for her book *Annie Allen*, making her the only black American ever to receive this award. The poem in this collection, "Gertrude," is from *Bronzeville Boys and Girls*.

Upon the death of Carl Sandburg, Ms. Brooks was named Poet Laureate of Illinois.

Besides writing, Ms. Brooks is active in teaching and lecturing throughout the country. Additional information on the poet's life and works can be found in her autobiography, *Report from Part One*.

Lucille Clifton was born in Depew, New York in 1936. She attended Howard University and Fredonia State Teachers College. She now lives in Baltimore, Maryland with her husband and six children.

Two books of her poetry include *Good Times* and *Good News About the Earth*. Ms. Clifton is also the author of several books for young children including *Some of the Days of Everett Anderson* and *Everett Anderson's Christmas Coming*. She has recently written the 1974 Summer Reading Bookmark Poem for the Children's Book Council's Summer Reading Program.

Linda Curry's poem, "For Nina Simone Wherever You Are," appears in *The Voice of the Children*, a collection of poems written by twenty-six youngsters between the ages of nine and seventeen who participated in a creative writing workshop in the Fort Greene section of Brooklyn, New York. Six other poems by Ms. Curry are also included in *The Voice of the Children*.

Mari Evans was born in Toledo, Ohio. Currently she lives in Indianapolis, Indiana where she is a writer-in-residence and visiting assistant professor in Black Literature at Indiana University in Bloomington.

The poems in this collection, "Who Can Be Born Black?" and "If There Be Sorrow" are from her book, *I Am a Black Woman*; which received the Black Academy of Arts and Letters Second Annual Poetry Award.

Nikki Giovanni was born in Knoxville, Tennessee in 1931 and raised in Cincinnati, Ohio. Graduated from Fisk University in 1967, she did graduate work at Columbia University and the University of Pennsylvania.

She has written several books of poems including *Spin a Soft Black Song*, a book of poems for children, and a recent adult book, *My House*. She can be heard reading her own work on two recordings, *Truth Is on Its Way* and *Like a Ripple on a Pond*.

Ms. Giovanni is one of the most powerful voices in the new black poetry movement. In 1973 she was the recipient of the Woman of the Year Award, sponsored by the *Ladies' Home Journal,* for youth leadership.

Michael S. Harper was born at home in Brooklyn, New York in 1938. His earliest artistic influence was jazz and the blues. He completed Master's degrees at both the University of Iowa Writer's Workshop and at California State University in Los Angeles. He taught for several years on the West Coast, and in 1970 joined the faculty of Brown University in Providence, Rhode Island.

His first book was *Dear John, Dear Coltrane,* a eulogy to the famous jazzman John Coltrane. This was followed by *History Is Your Own Heartbeat.* In 1971 he was a finalist for the National Book Award in poetry. His most recent publication is *Photographs: Negatives: History as Apple Tree.*

David Henderson was born in 1942 and raised in Harlem in New York City. After graduating from college he worked as a college teacher in New York. He now lives in Berkeley, California where he teaches, edits a magazine of black American literature called *Umbra/Blackworks,* and, of course, writes both poems and books.

Langston Hughes was born in Joplin, Missouri in 1902 and died in Harlem, New York City in 1967. During his lifelong writing career he created novels, short stories, plays, children's books, newspaper columns, operas, operettas, and, of course, poems.

Mr. Hughes graduated from Lincoln University in Pennsylvania and also attended Columbia University in New York City. He traveled widely throughout the United States, Europe and Africa. Many of the places he visited and the people he met provided inspiration for his writing.

You can read forty-five of his poems in the collection *Don't You Turn Back: Poems by Langston Hughes.* And you can read about the poet's exciting life in two biographies: *Langston Hughes: A Biography* by Milton Meltzer, and *Black Troubador: Langston Hughes* by Charlemae Hill Rollins.

Maurice Shelley Jackson.* The only information available on this author is that he attended Columbia High School in New York City.

Kojo Gyinaye Kyei was born in Ahafo, Ashanti and lived for a long time in Ghana. In 1956 he received a scholarship to come to the United States to study architecture at the University of Kansas. For many years he taught the Twi language to Peace Corps members studying to do work in Ghana.

Don L. Lee was born in Little Rock, Arkansas in 1942. He has taught Afro-American Literature and History at several colleges, including Cornell University in Ithaca, New York. Besides writing poetry, he is an important literary voice and has done several studies of black poets of the 1960's. Mr. Lee is also an editor of Third World Press, a black publishing company in Chicago, Illinois.

The poem in this collection, "The Cure All" is from his book *Black Pride,* published in 1968.

Naomi Long Madgett was born in Norfolk, Virginia, the youngest child of a Baptist minister. She studied at Virginia State College, Wayne State University, and the University of Detroit. Since 1946, she has lived in Detroit where she was an English teacher. In 1947 she was named Distinguished English Teacher of the Year. Since 1968 she has been an Associate Professor of English at Eastern Michigan University in Ypsilanti.

Her first book of poems, *Songs to a Phantom Nightingale,* appeared in 1941. The poem in this collection, "Midway," is from *Star by Star* published in 1965. Her most recent book of poetry, *Pink Ladies in the Afternoon,* appeared in 1972.

Raymond Richard Patterson was born in New York in 1929. He studied at Lincoln University and New York University. He teaches in New York and gives poetry readings throughout the state via the New York State Council on the Arts. A collection of his poetry, *26 Ways of Looking at a Black Man,* appeared in 1969.

Linda Porter.* The only information available on Ms. Porter is that she is from Chicago, Illinois.

Quandra Prettyman was born in Baltimore, Maryland. After graduating from Antioch College in Ohio, she studied at the University of Michigan. She has been an instructor in several colleges, including The New School for Social Research in New York, where she now lives and teaches English at Barnard College.

Dudley Randall was born in Washington, D.C. in 1914. He attended both Wayne State University and the University of Michigan, where he studied library science. He has been a librarian at Lincoln University in Missouri and Morgan College in Baltimore, Maryland.

Mr. Randall has published several volumes of poetry, including *More to Remember,* and has compiled several anthologies. He founded Broadside Press, a company devoted to publishing black American poetry.

Jo Nell Rice.* The only information to be found on Ms. Rice is that she attended Howard University Fine Arts School in Washington, D.C.

Richard Rive was born in 1931 in the heart of Cape Town, South Africa. In high school he became an outstanding track star. He currently teaches high school in Africa.

Yolande Zealy.* All that is known about Ms. Zealy is that she attended Howard University in Washington, D.C.

---

*The poems in this collection by Maurice Shelley Jackson, Linda Porter, Jo Nell Rice, and Yolande Zealy first appeared in the anthology *Cry at Birth,* a book of poems by black Americans ranging in age from ten to twenty-three years old, collected by The Bookers.

ABOUT THE AUTHOR

Lee Bennett Hopkins has had long experience as a teacher, lecturer, and educational consultant in school systems throughout the country. He is the author of numerous professional texts and children's books, including *Don't You Turn Back* and *City Talk* for Knopf.

Mr. Hopkins is currently a Curriculum and Editorial Specialist for Scholastic Book Services in New York City, and an instructor at the City College of New York.

ABOUT THE PHOTOGRAPHER

David Parks, a graduate of Rochester Institute of Technology, has been a professional freelance photographer since 1969. He is the author of a book, *GI Diary*, based on his experiences as a black soldier during two years of combat duty in Vietnam.

Mr. Parks lives in New York City, where he is at work directing his first feature-length motion picture.